The Crusades
Cultures in conflict

Pamela Kernaghan

Educational Adviser to the Order of St John

CAMBRIDGE
UNIVERSITY PRESS

Published by the Press Syndicate of the University of Cambridge
The Pitt Building, Trumpington Street, Cambridge CB2 1RP
40 West 20th Street, New York, NY 10011-4211, USA
10 Stamford Road, Oakleigh, Melbourne 3166, Australia

First published 1993

Printed in Great Britain at the University Press, Cambridge

A catalogue record for this book is available from the British Library

ISBN 0 521 44617 1 paperback

Picture research by Callie Kendall
Text illustrations by Sharon Pallent, Martin Sanders,
Sue Shields, Melanie Keogh, and Mark Peppé

Front cover illustration
Edimedia/Bibliothèque Nationale

Notice to teachers
Many of the sources used in this textbook have been adapted or abridged
from the original.

Acknowledgements
The publisher would like to make special acknowledgement to The Order of
St John for their sponsorship of the author during the writing of *The
Crusades* which was produced under the auspices of the London Centre for
the Study of the Crusades.

4, 25, 52, 55, By permission of the British Library, London; 5, 16, 21, 23,
48, Sonia Halliday/Bibliothèque Nationale; 9, 131, 20, 44, 45, 47t, 47b,
Order of St John; 10t, 36, Photo Biblioteca Vaticana; 10b, 17, 32, 54, 56,
British Library, London/ Bridgeman Art Library; 11, Alistair
Duncan/Middle East Archive; 12, 37, copyright British Museum; 13r, 19,
Ancient Art & Architecture Collection; 14, Michael Holford; 15,
Bibliothèque Royale Albert 1er; 24, 33, 41, Bibliothèque Nationale; 18,
Giraudon; 26, Bridgeman Art Library/Giraudon; 28, Bodleian Library, MS
Bodl. 264, f. 59r; 29, The Governing Body of Christ Church, Oxford; 30,
The Pierpont Morgan Library, New York, M240, f.8; 31, Screen Guides;
35t, Bridgeman–Giraudon; 35b, 40b, 49, Master & Fellows of Corpus
Christi College, Cambridge; 40t, The Corporation of London Records
Office/Order of St John; 42t, ©Warner Brothers/The Kobal Collection; 42b,
reproduced by permission of the House of Commons; 46, Michael Jenner;
50, The Bodleian Library, University of Oxford, MS Laud. Misc. 752, f.
146r; 59, E.T. Archive; 60, Sonia Halliday/British Library, London; 61, The
Bodleian Library, University of Oxford, MS Pococke 375, f. 3/4

Contents

Introduction

Spies report strange news

In the year 1096 one of the most powerful Muslim rulers in Asia Minor was given strange news by his spies. They told him of the approach of thousands of people from the West, all wearing the symbol of the cross on their clothes. This was the beginning of the crusades.

What were the crusades and do they still matter today?

Kilij Arslan was the first Muslim ruler to be told of the approach of the Franks. He was used to hearing about soldiers who had journeyed from western Europe to the East to sell their services to anyone willing to pay. But these Franks (West Europeans) were different. It was August 1096 and this time, along with the knights and foot-soldiers, there were thousands of men, women, children and old people, all wearing strips of cloth in the shape of a cross sewn on to their clothes. Why were so many people, most of whom were not soldiers or knights, such a long way from their homes? Where were they going and why were they wearing crosses?

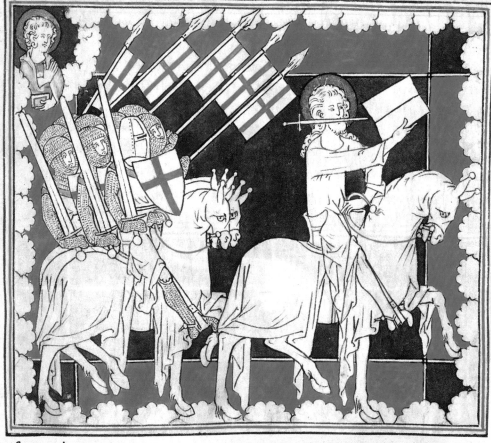

Source A
This fourteenth-century picture shows Christ leading crusaders.

• *Is the artist for or against crusades? How can you tell?*

4

The spies of Kilij Arslan had seen the beginning of a movement that was to last for hundreds of years. Christians, wearing the symbol of the cross, took part in crusades, or holy wars, against those whom they believed were the enemies of Christ. The main enemies were Muslims but there were also pagans, Jews and some Christians.

The idea of crusading was so popular and important in western Europe in the Middle Ages that most people were involved in some way and many thousands of men, women and children actually 'took the cross', which meant they promised God they would go on crusade. Rich and poor left their jobs, homes and families. They set out knowing that crusading could cost them everything they had, it would be dangerous and unpleasant, and they might never return. Were these the same people who were greedy, cruel and violent?

Source B
A fourteenth-century drawing of the siege of Jerusalem in 1099.
• *Could you learn anything from this about what the siege was really like?*

Source C

An eye-witness describes what he saw after Christians captured Jerusalem in 1099.

'In all the streets and squares of the city, mounds of heads, hands and feet were to be seen. People were walking quite openly over dead men and horses. But I have as yet described only the minor horrors . . . if I described what I actually saw you would not believe me.'

The History of Raymond of Aguilers, written before 1105

Source D

An Arab historian tells us:

'It is often surprising to discover how much the attitude of the Arabs, and Muslims in general, towards the West is still influenced, even today, by events that supposedly ended centuries ago.'

Amin Maalouf, *The Crusades Through Arab Eyes,* 1983

found today. For Muslims, the memory of the medieval crusades against them also still matters.

In this book you will find out about and investigate many different aspects of the crusades. Through your study you will learn about events that not only changed the history of Europe but are important in our own time too.

When calls were made for crusades against Muslims, the language of hate was used to stir people up and persuade them to take the cross. The crusades ended but there is evidence that the fear and hatred Christians were encouraged to feel about Muslims then can still be

The First Crusade was proclaimed by Pope Urban II in 1095. The crusader armies that set off the following year were defeated and never reached Palestine. Finally, in 1099, a crusader army captured Jerusalem.

Muslim forces had grown stronger and recaptured land from the Christians. As a result the Second Crusade was proclaimed in 1145. The main crusade was to the East but there was also fighting in Portugal, Spain and the Baltic. The crusaders in the East were defeated outside Damascus.

In 1187 Saladin recaptured Jerusalem and the Third Crusade was proclaimed. Three powerful crusader armies set off including that of Richard of England. Jerusalem was not taken but a treaty between Saladin and Richard allowed the Christians to keep control of part of the coast of Palestine.

1095   1145   1187 1198 1244
                   1212 1213

1050   1100   1150   1200   1250

In another attempt to recapture Jerusalem the Fourth Crusade was launched in 1198. The aim was to attack Egypt, centre of Muslim power. However, the main crusader army went off course and captured the Christian city of Constantinople.

In the thirteenth century, crusades were launched against Egypt. The Fifth and Sixth Crusades were proclaimed in 1213 and 1244. Both invaded Egypt but were defeated.

There were many other crusades including the Children's Crusade of 1212 and the Shepherds' Crusade of 1251. After the fall of Acre in 1291 the Muslim victory was complete but this did not end the crusades. They were still being proclaimed in the sixteenth century and even after.

1350   1400   1450   1500   1550

Jerusalem – Holy City

The crusades were Christian holy wars fought against people of different beliefs and different religions. One of the most important aims of the crusaders was to capture the city of Jerusalem and keep it under Christian rule.

What were the different religions and why was Jerusalem so important?

Europe & the Middle East A.D. 1090

Baltic Sea

PAGAN LANDS

London

Paris

WESTERN CHRISTIAN

Clermont

EASTERN CHRISTIAN

Black Sea

Manzikert
(Seljuk victory 1071)

Lisbon

Rome

Constantinople

Seljuk advances

Granada

Nicaea

Armenia

Edessa

Asia Minor

Antioch

Persia

Tunis

Middle East

Mediterranean Sea

Acre

Jerusalem

North Africa

Arabia

Muslim rule

Byzantine Empire

Armenian Christian

0   500   1000 km

Mecca

A model of the Church of the Holy Sepulchre in Jerusalem. The Church was built on the spot where Christians believed Christ was buried and then rose from the dead.

Jesus Christ is, for Christians, the son of God. He was born, lived and died in Palestine, which was then under the control of the Romans. He was a Jew who taught that Jewish leaders at the time were not following the laws of God, his father. The leaders did not accept that Jesus was the son of God. When he preached in the city of Jerusalem, the most holy place for Jews, he was arrested. He was tried by the Romans and crucified at Calvary, just outside the city walls.

The followers of Jesus believed that he was the Messiah, or Christ, which means that he was God on Earth, and these Christians set out to spread the new religion. About 300 years later, in the fourth century, the Roman Emperor Constantine became a Christian. Before long the whole Roman Empire was Christian, but it was an empire in two parts.

The Eastern or Byzantine Empire was ruled from Constantinople, a city which had been called Byzantium and was renamed by Constantine. Here Eastern Christians came to do some things differently from Western Christians, whose leader was the Pope in Rome. The churches and religious pictures looked different, and the way people worshipped was different. The Eastern Church and the Western Church argued about which was more truly Christian and which should be more powerful. Some of these arguments continue to the present day.

Source B

An eleventh-century Byzantine mosaic showing the Emperor Alexius Comnenus. The figure of Christ is making the sign of the cross in the way it is still made by Eastern Orthodox Christians.

Not everyone in Europe was Christian. There were communities of Jews who, after a revolt against the Romans, had been driven out of Palestine. There were other peoples who were pagan and worshipped many different gods. In the seventh century the Christians, Jews and pagans of Europe were joined by a new religious group, Muslims.

The Prophet Muhammad was born in the city of Mecca (which Muslims refer to as Makkah), in Arabia, in about AD 570. People in Arabia worshipped many gods and Muhammad taught that there is only one true God, Allah. The new religion was Islam, which means 'submission to God' and its followers were Muslims which means 'people who have submitted to God'.

Source C

A map of the world produced in England in the thirteenth century.

• *Which city is shown as being at the centre of the world?*

Islam was spreading during Muhammad's lifetime. Soon Arab Muslims had conquered many lands and spread Islam throughout North Africa and into Europe. They also conquered Palestine and the city of Jerusalem. It was from here that Muslims believe that the Prophet Muhammad rose to heaven. On that holy place was built the Dome of the Rock.

So Jerusalem is a unique city: it is holy for three of the world's great religions. For Jews it is their ancient capital, where, thousands of years ago, King Solomon built his temple, part of which still survives. For Christians it is the place where Jesus was crucified and rose from the dead. For Muslims it is the city from which Muhammad rose to heaven.

Muslims ruled Jerusalem and Palestine, the Holy Land, from the seventh century and, for most of that time, Jews and Christians were free to live, travel and worship. But in the eleventh century great changes took place and a new era in the history of Europe began: the era of crusading.

Source D
The Dome of the Rock in Jerusalem. It is built on the spot from which Muslims believe Muhammad rose to heaven.

1 Each of the following is marked on the map on page 8:

Jerusalem   **Paris**
Granada   **Nicaea**
Pagan lands   **Tunis**

Match each name to one of these regions:

North Africa   **Asia Minor**
The Baltic   **The Middle East**
Western Europe

2 Having read the unit, which of the following statements do you agree with?
- Muslim armies conquered parts of Europe.
- The Christian Church was divided.
- There were only Muslims and Christians in Europe.
- Eastern Christians were ruled from Rome.

3 Jerusalem is holy for Jews, Christians and Muslims. Write a few lines explaining why it is a holy city for three religions.

Changes in the East

In the eleventh century great changes took place in the East. The armies of a people called the Seljuk Turks had ridden out from their homeland of Persia. They attacked and conquered many lands, some Christian and some Muslim.

What were the effects of the Seljuk conquests?

Kilij Arslan, the first Muslim ruler to be told of the approach of the Franks, was a Seljuk Turk. His people had been converted to Islam less than one hundred years before. In about 1040 their armies began to invade lands from Persia to the Mediterranean Sea, and their name was soon heard with fear. These Muslim warriors conquered vast areas and became very powerful.

At that time the Seljuk Turks were a nomadic, illiterate people, and they have left no written accounts of their invasions. Nor did any eye-witnesses among the survivors of the invasions write about their experiences. We have to learn what we can from people who wrote some time later.

Source A

Armenia was a Christian country which had been part of the Byzantine Empire. Matthew of Edessa, an Armenian, wrote this description of its conquest by Seljuk Turks.

'The Greeks [Byzantines], whose claim to fame and glory rests on the speed with which they run away, had destroyed our army and left us unprotected. The Persian Turks poured in and in a year reached the gates of Constantinople itself. Who would be strong enough to tell of Armenia's suffering? Blood flowed everywhere and the mountains and hills were trampled underfoot as the hooves of the infidels' horses destroyed them. The smell given off by the dead bodies spread infection far and wide. Persia overflowed with captives; carnivores feasted on corpses.'

Chronicle of Matthew of Edessa, about 1140

Source B
A Seljuk warrior shown on a thirteenth-century dish.

Source C

Anna Comnena was born in 1083. She was the daughter of the Byzantine emperor, Alexius Comnenus, and wrote a biography of her father. In it she describes how close the Seljuk Turks came to the Byzantine capital, Constantinople.

'At this time the godless Turks were . . . sending out raiders to devastate all the country . . . they came on horses and on foot even as far as the Bosphorus, and carried off much booty . . . The Byzantines saw them living fearlessly in all the little towns along the coasts . . . nobody drove them out for the inhabitants were absolutely panic-stricken and did not know what steps to take.'

Anna Comnena, *The Alexiad*, about 1140

The Seljuk Turks reached the height of their power in the 1070s when they defeated the Byzantine army at the Battle of Manzikert. But it was not only the Christian Empire in the East that was in danger. Other Muslim rulers were also attacked. Most of Palestine, including Jerusalem, fell to the Seljuks and the Middle East was in great disorder.

Source F

This Seljuk coin shows the zodiac sign, Sagittarius. It was minted in Sivas in Turkey.

Source D

A twelfth-century painted window from the abbey of St Denys in France. It shows crusaders pursuing Seljuks.

• *What impression is it meant to give you about Seljuks?*

Source E

Anna Comnena married Nicephorus Bryennius. Just before he died Nicephorus wrote this description of what happened at the time of the Seljuk invasions.

'At this time a Greek [Byzantine] nobleman . . . who claimed the empire, drew on to his side Turkish troops and leaders and toured the cities of Asia. The cities submitted to him and surrendered their towns to him as if he were emperor, and he . . . handed them over to the Turks.'

Nicephorus Bryennius, *Histories*, written about 1130

Soon after their great victories, quarrels broke out between Seljuk rulers. In Kilij Arslan's family, brother killed brother and cousin killed cousin. These quarrels meant that, as the Franks approached, the Seljuk Turks were not united.

1 None of the people writing about the Seljuk invasions was an eye-witness. Does this mean that we cannot trust what they have written?

2 Based on the sources in this unit, which author or authors would agree with each of these statements:
• Some Byzantines were traitors.
• The Seljuks killed many people.
• Byzantines did not fight back strongly.

3 What can you learn from Source B about how Seljuks fought?

4 Many things changed as a result of the Seljuk invasions. One change was that Armenia was no longer in the Byzantine Empire. What other changes can you find?

Changes in the West

3

In Europe in the eleventh century life was usually hard and violent. Many people who called themselves Christians did not behave well or obey the Church. Church leaders tried to change people's behaviour by encouraging pilgrimages, particularly to the Holy City of Jerusalem. But changes in the East had made pilgrimages dangerous.

Why would pilgrimages change people's behaviour and what had happened to make pilgrimages to Jerusalem dangerous?

In Europe in the twentieth century there have been years of terrible war and also years of peace. In eleventh-century Europe, few people had a peaceful lifetime. Violent attack and death could come at any time. The population was growing rapidly and there were fears that there would not be enough land and food to go around. People fought to protect what they had and to add to it, if they could. The most powerful people were the nobles and the knights and, because they thought they had the most to lose, they were the most violent of all. For many, violence and killing were a way of life and they trusted only their own family and their feudal lord.

Source A
According to a writer of the time, Pope Urban II was very angry at the behaviour of knights and said:

'Listen and understand. You have strapped on the belt of knighthood and strut with pride in your eye. You butcher your brothers and create factions among yourselves. This . . . is not the knighthood of Christ . . . you are not following the path that leads to life. You oppressors of orphans, you robbers of widows, you murderers, you blasphemers.'

Pope Urban II, according to Baldric of Bourgueil, writing in about 1108

Source B
A section of the Bayeux Tapestry, made after the Norman invasion of England in 1066. It shows the arms and armour used by knights in the eleventh century.

In the eleventh century, the Christian Church wanted to make people behave in less violent ways and therefore encouraged pilgrimages to holy places. Pilgrims had to go through a long, difficult and dangerous journey to reach the holy place. Their suffering was a way of showing God that they were trying to make up for the sins they had committed. The greatest Christian pilgrimage was to Jerusalem in Palestine. Jerusalem is also holy for Jews and Muslims and, since the seventh century, it had been under Muslim rulers. Christian pilgrims and Christian holy places were, for most of those hundreds of years, respected and protected by those rulers. However, when Urban II was pope, law and order had broken down in many parts of Palestine as the Seljuk Turks carried out their conquests. No one, including Christian pilgrims, was safe from attack and Church leaders wanted Jerusalem to be made safe for pilgrims. They also believed that the city in which Christ had died and risen from the dead should be ruled by Christians.

Source C

A guide book for pilgrims, written in the twelfth century, reminds us why Jerusalem was so holy for Christians.

'The sepulchre [tomb] of our Lord Jesus Christ is in the middle of the Temple of the Holy Sepulchre ... Further east is the Centre of the World. Not far from that ... is Mount Calvary, on which the Lord was crucified.'

Source D ▲

A twelfth-century map showing Jerusalem and its location. The Holy City is shown as a perfect circle and is divided into four quarters. The signs of a Christian pilgrim were a scrip (small bag) and a staff. Pilgrims who had been to Jerusalem also carried a palm frond (leaf).

• *Who are the people shown on the map? How can you identify them?*

---

1 You are a historian who wants to find out about knights in the eleventh century.
a Which sources might be useful to you?
b What does each of the sources you have chosen tell you about knights?
c Think of some questions about knights that these sources do not help you to answer. What could you do to find out the answers to your questions?

2 Work in pairs. One of you is a knight explaining why he behaves in a violent way. The other is a monk trying to persuade the knight to change his behaviour and go on a pilgrimage to Jerusalem. Write down what each might say.

Crusading is launched

In the year 1095 Pope Urban II spoke to a gathering in the French city of Clermont. The Pope was the leader of all the Christians in western Europe and what he had to say was very important. He called on people to take part in what is now known as the First Crusade.

Why did the Pope proclaim a crusade and how were people persuaded to take part?

We do not know what Pope Urban actually said but there are reports of his speech written afterwards by people who heard it.

Source A

Fulcher of Chartres was one of those eye-witnesses and here is part of what he wrote down as the words of Pope Urban:

'As many of you have already been told, the Turks, a Persian race, have overrun the Christians right up to the Mediterranean Sea. Occupying more and more of the lands of the Christians on the borders of Romania [the Byzantine Empire], they have conquered them . . . slaughtering and capturing many, destroying churches and laying waste the Kingdom of God. So if you leave them alone much longer they will further grind under their heels the faithful of God.'

Pope Urban II, according to the *History of Fulcher of Chartres*, 1105

Source B

Pope Urban II visits the abbey of Cluny about a month before he spoke at Clermont. Urban had been Grand Prior of Cluny before he became Pope. From a twelfth-century manuscript.

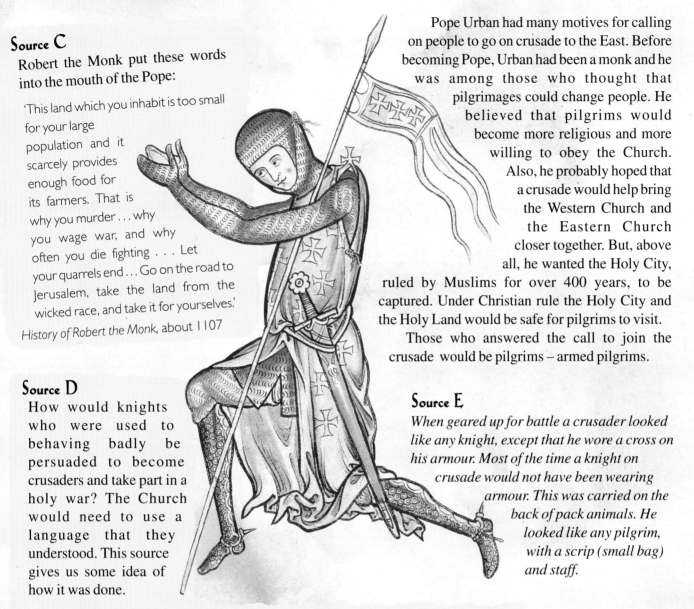

Source C

Robert the Monk put these words into the mouth of the Pope:

'This land which you inhabit is too small for your large population and it scarcely provides enough food for its farmers. That is why you murder . . . why you wage war, and why often you die fighting . . . Let your quarrels end . . . Go on the road to Jerusalem, take the land from the wicked race, and take it for yourselves.'

History of Robert the Monk, about 1107

Source D

How would knights who were used to behaving badly be persuaded to become crusaders and take part in a holy war? The Church would need to use a language that they understood. This source gives us some idea of how it was done.

'I address fathers and sons and brothers and nephews. If an outsider were to strike any of your kin down, would you not avenge your blood relative? How much more ought you to avenge your God, your father, your brother whom you see banished from his estates, crucified!'

A sermon preached to crusaders just before the capture of Jerusalem, according to Baldric of Bourgueil, writing in about 1108

Pope Urban had many motives for calling on people to go on crusade to the East. Before becoming Pope, Urban had been a monk and he was among those who thought that pilgrimages could change people. He believed that pilgrims would become more religious and more willing to obey the Church. Also, he probably hoped that a crusade would help bring the Western Church and the Eastern Church closer together. But, above all, he wanted the Holy City, ruled by Muslims for over 400 years, to be captured. Under Christian rule the Holy City and the Holy Land would be safe for pilgrims to visit.

Those who answered the call to join the crusade would be pilgrims – armed pilgrims.

Source E

When geared up for battle a crusader looked like any knight, except that he wore a cross on his armour. Most of the time a knight on crusade would not have been wearing armour. This was carried on the back of pack animals. He looked like any pilgrim, with a scrip (small bag) and staff.

Here are some of the possible motives (reasons why) Pope Urban II launched the First Crusade:

- to stop knights fighting each other
- to make himself more powerful
- to protect Christians in the Byzantine Empire
- to capture Jerusalem
- to make the Holy Land safe for pilgrims
- to acquire land.

1 Find evidence in the sources that each of these was a motive of the Pope.

2 Can you find evidence for any other motives that he had?

3 Make a list of all the motives you have found evidence for. Put them in what you think would be their order of importance to the Pope. Explain why you chose that order.

The First Crusade

Nearly four years after Pope Urban II proclaimed the First Crusade, Christian armies broke through the walls of the city of Jerusalem.

What happened during the First Crusade?

The Franks with crosses sewn on to their clothes who so puzzled Kilij Arslan were men and women who had responded to the call of Pope Urban II. This was the first wave of people who had taken the cross and made their crusader vow.

Pope Urban had given a date, 15 August 1096, for the Crusade to begin but some ignored this and set out earlier. The most famous leader of this first wave of crusaders was Peter the Hermit who had been preaching and gathering followers since the Pope spoke at Clermont. In April, he and thousands of followers set off. Most of these men and women were peasants although, as Kilij Arslan was told, there were also some knights with them.

There was disorder and trouble from the beginning. In parts of France and Germany, Jews were attacked and killed. You will learn more about this in Unit 9.

As the crusaders moved on into eastern Europe there was fighting with local people. In Europe there had been bad harvests and there were near-famine conditions. Thousands of hungry people moving eastwards with few supplies of their own were not welcome in many places. Crusaders fought and pillaged for food, attacking homes, villages and towns along their route to Constantinople. Those of Peter's followers who carried on into Asia Minor were defeated and slaughtered by the army of Kilij Arslan in October 1096.

Source A

A thirteenth-century illustration of Peter the Hermit preaching the First Crusade.

Some lessons were learned from this disaster. The next wave of crusaders heading east were better supplied and better organised. They left after the date set by the Pope and after the best harvest in Europe for years. This meant that there was less fear of starvation and less reason for disorder.

There were four main armies each under different leaders and following different routes. The leaders were mostly French and included Hugh, a brother of the King of France, and Robert of Normandy, son of William the Conqueror. These armies gathered in Constantinople in early 1097.

The first target of the crusaders was Nicaea, chief city of Kilij Arslan and home to his wife and family. He was away fighting a rival Muslim ruler when, in June, the attack began. He returned swiftly but could not break through the Christian forces, and he withdrew. This was the first important crusader victory but they were still a long way from Jerusalem.

The next city that the crusaders planned to take was Antioch and the journey there was terrible. The land had already been laid waste by the Turkish invasions and there was little food or water. It was the height of summer and people and animals died in great numbers.

Source C

The Siege of Nicaea. Kilij Arslan's wife was captured by the crusaders as she tried to escape from the besieged city.

Source B

An eye-witness described the journey to Antioch.

'We... began to cross a mountain, which was so high and steep that none of our men dared to overtake another on the mountain path. Horses fell over the precipice, and one beast of burden dragged another down. As for the knights, they stood about in a great state of gloom, wringing their hands because they were so frightened and miserable, not knowing what to do with themselves and their armour.

We went through a land which was deserted, waterless and uninhabitable, from which we barely emerged or escaped alive for we suffered greatly from hunger and thirst, and found nothing at all to eat except prickly plants which we gathered and rubbed between our hands.'

Gesta Francorum [The Deeds of the Franks], written during the First Crusade

Knights were trained to fight on horseback, and pack horses were needed to carry arms and armour. By the time Antioch was reached, in October 1097, there were 5,000 knights and fewer than 1,000 horses. By the following summer there were fewer than 200 horses and even leaders like Godfrey of Bouillon and Robert of Flanders had to beg for horses for themselves.

The Muslim forces defended Antioch against the crusader siege for over seven months. In that time the 40,000 men and women in the crusader armies were constantly under attack and close to starvation. The city fell only after one of the defenders turned traitor and helped the crusaders break through.

This was far from the end of the crusaders' problems. They were now inside Antioch and under siege themselves from a Muslim army. Conditions were so bad and morale so low that the gates had to be sealed to stop deserters from leaving. At last it was decided that there was little choice but to march out and fight. The result was a victory so surprising that crusaders believed they had been joined by a heavenly army of angels, saints and dead crusaders.

Source D
- *What problems did crusaders face crossing land such as this on the route to Antioch?*

Source E

The siege of Antioch from a thirteenth-century manuscript.

- *What do you notice about how the knights are drawn?*

After more troubles including an epidemic, probably of typhoid, the march to Jerusalem continued. The crusaders were passing through lands where the Muslim rulers were more interested in fighting each other and the Turks than in attacking Christians. They reached Jerusalem in June 1099 and, after a siege lasting six weeks, broke through the wall. The news of the Christian victory swept through Europe. It came, however, too late for Pope Urban II, who died on 29 July 1099.

Source F

The same eye-witness who wrote about the journey wrote this description of what happened when Jerusalem fell.

'Our men all entered the City, and each seized his share of whatever goods he found in houses and cellars, and when it was dawn they killed everyone, man or woman, that they met in any place whatsoever.'

Gesta Francorum, written during the First Crusade

---

1 According to this account of the First Crusade, in what order did the following events happen?

- The son of William the Conqueror arrives in Constantinople.

- Crusaders led by Peter the Hermit are wiped out.

- Jerusalem falls to the crusaders.

- The journey from Nicaea to Antioch.

- Typhoid strikes crusaders.

- The capture of Kilij Arslan's wife.

2 Source B is a description of part of the journey, written by an eye-witness. Source E shows crusaders attacking Antioch.

a Do the sources give different impressions of knights?

b If they do, does that mean one of the sources is false?

3 Can you tell what feelings the writer of Source F had about what happened when Jerusalem fell? What do you think about how the description is written?

6 The crusader states

After the First Crusade the parts of the Middle East conquered by the Christians were divided into four states, the largest of which was the Kingdom of Jerusalem. Some people – although not many – who went on crusade stayed and settled in these Christian or crusader states.

What was life like for the Muslims and Christians living in the crusader states?

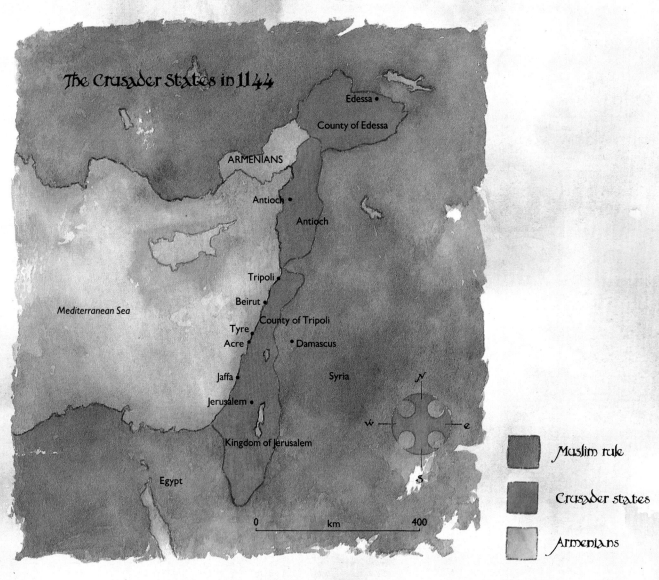

The Crusader States in 1144

Edessa •

County of Edessa

ARMENIANS

Antioch •

Antioch

Tripoli •

Beirut •

Mediterranean Sea

County of Tripoli

Tyre •

Acre •

• Damascus

Jaffa •

Syria

N

Jerusalem •

W

E

Kingdom of Jerusalem

S

Egypt

0   km   400

Muslim rule

Crusader states

Armenians

Source A

Ibn Jubayr, a Muslim, described some of his experiences when travelling with a caravan in the Kingdom of Jerusalem.

'Our way lay through continuous farms and ordered settlements, whose inhabitants were all Muslims, living comfortably with the Franks. God protect us from such temptation. They surrender half their crops to the Franks at harvest time, and pay as well a poll-tax of one dinar and five qirats for each person. Other than that they are not interfered with, save for a light tax on the fruits of trees. Their horses and all their effects are left to their full possession ... On the same Monday we alighted at a farmstead a parasang [about 5.5 kilometres] distance from Acre. Its headman is a Muslim appointed by the Franks to oversee the Muslim workers in it ... when we came to Acre we were taken to the custom-house ... Before the door are stone benches, spread with carpets, where are the Christian clerks of the Customs with their ebony ink-stands ornamented with gold. They write Arabic, which they also speak.'

Ibn Jubayr, who travelled in the crusader states in about 1180

Source B

A settler from France, Fulcher of Chartres, wrote about the lives and attitudes of the settlers that he knew.

'We used to be Westerners; now we are Easterners. You may once have been a Roman or a Frenchman; here, and now, you are a Galilean or a Palestinian. For we have forgotten the lands of our birth; to most of us they are now strange, foreign countries. Some ... are married not only to girls from back home, but also to Syrians, Armenians and even Muslims – but of course only to baptised ones.'

The History of Fulcher of Chartres, about 1108

Source C

The travellers Abu Zayd and al-Harith arrive in a village with their caravan.

- *What exactly is this type of 'caravan'?*

Source D

Source E

Usamah ibn-Munqidh was the son of the Lord of Shaizar in northern Syria. Shaizar was close to the crusader states and Usamah met many Franks on his travels. When he was nearly 90 years old, he wrote his memoirs. In them he tells this story about a Frankish knight with whom he had made friends.

'When he decided to return by sea to his homeland he said to me: "My brother, I am leaving for my country and I want you to send your son with me (my son was then 14 years old) to our country, where he can see the knights and learn wisdom and chivalry. When he returns he will be like a wise man." Even if my son were to be taken captive, this could not be a worse misfortune than carrying him into the land of the Franks. However, I said to the man: "By your life, this has been exactly my idea. But the only thing that prevented me from carrying it out was that his grandmother, my mother, is so fond of him and did not let him come out with me until I had sworn an oath . . . that I would return him to her." "Well", said he, "disobey her not."'

Usamah ibn-Munquidh, *Kitab al-i 'tibar* [translated as An Arab-Syrian Gentleman and Warrior in the Period of the Crusades], written in the 1180s

---

1 According to Source A,
a how had rule by the Franks changed life for Muslims?
b in what ways had life not changed?

2 Do you believe Fulcher of Chartres (Source B) when he says, 'We used to be Westerners; now we are Easterners'?

3 You are researching relations between Christians and Muslims in the crusader states. You have come across Source D but have no information about it. What do you need to know about the source before you can tell whether it will be useful to you?

4 In your own words, tell the story told by Usamah ibn-Munqidh in Source E.

7 The call to crusade

In western Europe the crusades had an impact on almost everyone's life. Those who did not take the cross themselves would probably know someone who did. Most people would go to listen to the sermons of crusade preachers, and everyone had to pay taxes for crusades.

How did crusades begin and how were they paid for?

We live in a world which is, in many ways, different from the world of people who went on crusade. When we try to learn about and understand their lives and experiences we must remember those differences. How can we know what it was like to live at that time? The people are no longer around to tell us. But we can still ask questions and, like historians, study what remains behind from the past: the historical record.

How did a crusade begin?

A crusade was always proclaimed by a pope, who was believed to be carrying out the will of God.

Source A

After a great Muslim victory at the Battle of Hattin, and the recapture of Jerusalem, this is how the Third Crusade was proclaimed.

'The Lord's cross was taken, the bishops were slain, the King was captured and almost everyone was either killed by the sword or seized . . . What a great cause for mourning this ought to be for us and the whole Christian people . . . let us in no way hesitate to do for God what the infidels do not fear to attempt against the Lord.'

Pope Gregory VIII, *Letter of Proclamation of the Third Crusade,* 1187

Source B

St Louis, King of France, setting out with his knights on crusade in 1270. He is being followed by a procession of monks.

• *The words 'Dieu le veut' were used about the beginning of a new crusade. What do these words mean?*

25

After the letter had been sent out, crusade preachers travelled from place to place giving sermons to persuade people to take the cross.

St Bernard of Clairvaux was one of the most successful crusade preachers. He travelled widely to gain support for the Second Crusade, which was proclaimed after Muslim forces recaptured Edessa (look back to the map on page 22).

(look back to the map on page 22).

Source C

In 1146, at Vezelay in France, huge crowds gathered to hear St Bernard preach the Second Crusade. An eye-witness describes the effect of his preaching.

'With loud outcry people on every side began to demand crosses. And when he [St Bernard] had sowed, rather than distributed, the parcel of crosses which had been prepared beforehand, he was forced to tear his own garments into crosses.'

Odo of Deuil, 1148

Source D

We do not know exactly what St Bernard said when he preached but he wrote many letters and books. Here he is writing about the rewards that God would give to crusaders.

'God arranges for himself to be in need, or pretends to be, so that he can award wages to those fighting for him: the remission of their sins and everlasting glory ... make sure not to let the chance pass you by. Take the sign of the cross and you will obtain ... remission of all the sins which you have confessed.'

St Bernard of Clairvaux, twelfth century

Source E

This drawing, from a twelfth-century manuscript, shows St Bernard preaching.
• Can you work out which letter of the alphabet this drawing is a part of?

How were crusades paid for?

In the early years of crusading, crusaders had to pay their own costs unless a richer person agreed to help. Taking part in a crusade cost a lot of money and, to raise it, land usually had to be sold or pledged. To avoid these problems, everyone was made to pay special taxes.

1 Study Sources C and D. In your own words,
a explain what happened at Vezelay.

b explain the rewards St Bernard claimed God would give to crusaders.

2 With a vertical rule, divide a page into two parts. On one side write down reasons why people took the cross when St Bernard preached. Next to each reason give the evidence you found for it in this unit.

3 Does what happened at Vezelay remind you of anything you have seen or heard about in the world today?

Leaving home

Many people went on crusade leaving their family behind.

What did they feel about leaving home and what were the effects on their families?

Most people in western Europe in the Middle Ages were illiterate, so we only have evidence about the feelings of those people who could write.

Source A

John of Joinville went on crusade with King Louis of France and wrote this description of his departure in 1248.

'The abbot of Cheminon gave me my scrip [purse] and staff. And then I left Joinville, not to enter the castle again until my return . . . as I went . . . I never once looked back towards Joinville for fear that my heart would be moved because of the beautiful castle I was leaving and my two children.'

History of John of Joinville, early fourteenth century

Source B

It is not known who wrote this poem or when it was written.

'Good Lord God, if I for you
Leave the country where she is that I love so,
Grant us in heaven everlasting joy,
My love and me, through your mercy,
And grant her the strength to love me,
So that she will not forget me in my long absence,
For I love her more than anything in the world
And I feel so sad about her that my heart is breaking.'

Source C

A medieval image of romance, from a fourteenth-century manuscript.

• *What impression do you get about the man's attitude to the woman?*

Both women and men went on crusade and there is evidence that at least one woman fought in a crusader army. Sometimes a husband and wife would go on crusade together but more often the wife and family were left behind when a man went on crusade.

Source E
Women defending a castle. From a fourteenth-century English manuscript.

• *What weapons are the women shown using?*

Source D
Baha' ad-Din, an adviser to Saladin, wrote the following:

'Behind their rampart . . . there was a woman wrapped in a green melluta [shawl], who kept on shooting arrows from a wooden bow, with which she wounded several of our men. She was at last overpowered by numbers; we killed her and brought the bow she had been using to the Sultan [Saladin], who was greatly astonished.'

Baha' ad-Din, *Biography of Saladin*, early thirteenth century

The following information, taken from different historical records, tells us about some people's experiences.

1190 Six weeks after William Trussel went on crusade, his wife was murdered by his half-brother.

1208 Reginald of Sugestaple and his wife mortgaged their land to raise money to go on crusade. When they returned, their land had been sold and they could not get it back.

1220 William Luvel married Cecilia. William was already married and Cecilia's husband was alive and on crusade.

1249 Walter the Tailor sold everything, including his wife's dowry, to go on crusade. His wife, Christian, was left with nothing.

1268 Margaret's husband was killed on crusade. So much had been sold that she had nothing left to pay his debts.

Source F

Blanche of Castile and her son, King Louis IX of France, from a thirteenth-century manuscript.

• *Why do you think historians know a lot about Blanche?*

It is important to remember that many women did not have these experiences and, left on their own, managed as well as or better than their husbands or sons. The records give little evidence about such women, although there are exceptions. For example, much is known about Blanche of Castile. She was the mother of King Louis IX of France and ruled the country in his place when he went on crusade.

1 We only have evidence for the feelings of people who could write. Does this make a difference to what we can know about the past?

2 Sources C, E and F give different images of women. Use at least three words which you think best describe each image.

3 Study the examples, taken from historical records, of what happened to some of the people who were left behind. Can you work out what sort of records these examples came from?

4 Why do these records not help us to find out about women who managed well when they were left on their own?

5 Some historians are trying to find out more about women. Could such knowledge make a difference to people's ideas about the past?

6 You are a journalist researching for an article with the title 'Women's experiences during the crusades'. Use the evidence from this unit, and any other part of the book, to help you write notes for your article.

9 Victims of crusades

For hundreds of years the lives of millions of people – Christians, Jews, Muslims and pagans – were affected by the crusades. Many of these were victims who suffered greatly at the hands of crusaders.

What happened to people who were victims of the crusades?

Jews were victims of the crusaders from the beginning of crusading.

Source A

One historian wrote this account of what happened to thousands of Jewish people living in Germany during the First Crusade.

'They travelled east through the Rhineland, where they came upon communities of Jews. Suddenly these soldiers of the cross who were pledged to travel thousands of miles to fight Muslims, realised that they had "infidels" in their own lands. Why spare the "murderers of the Lord"? Ferociously the crusaders attacked the Jewish sections of town after town: Cologne, Worms, Mainz . . . They left behind them charred ruins and bodies of some 5,000 massacred men, women and children.'

From an adaptation by David Bamberger of Abba Eban's *History of the Jews*, 1979.

Source B

A thirteenth-century bible illustration showing Jews being massacred.

• *Is the artist for or against the killings?*

Source C

This piece is adapted from a description written at the time, in Hebrew, of what a Jewish woman did rather than have her children taken and forced to become Christians.

'Rachel took Isaac her small son and slaughtered him. The lad, Aaron, when he saw that his brother had been slaughtered cried out, "Mother, mother, do not slaughter me!" He then went and hid himself under a table. She took her two daughters, Bella and Matrona, and sacrificed them to the Lord God of Hosts. She then lifted her voice and called out to her son. She pulled him by the leg from under the table and sacrificed him. She then put them under her two sleeves, two on one side and two on the other, near her heart. The crusaders found her sitting and mourning them. They said to her, "Show us the money you have under your sleeves." When they saw the slaughtered children, they killed her.'

Hebrew Chronicle of the First Crusade, written at the time

According to Arab chroniclers, both Muslims and Jews were victims when Jerusalem was captured by Christians in 1099.

Source D

'The population of the holy city was put to the sword, and the Franks spent a week massacring Muslims. They killed more than 70,000 people in al-Aqsa mosque.'

Ibn al-Athir, *The Collection of Histories*, about 1220

Source E

'Many people were killed. The Jews had gathered in their synagogue and the Franks burned them alive.'

Ibn al-Qalanisi, *Chronicle of Damascus*, about 1160

Source F

A Christian eye-witness wrote this.

'Once the city had been captured it was most rewarding to see the devotion of the pilgrims before the Holy Sepulchre: how they clapped in joy, singing a new song to the Lord.'

The History of Raymond of Aguilers, written before 1105

Source G
Many massacres were carried out by crusaders. Thirteenth-century drawing.

Eastern Christians of the Byzantine Empire were also victims.

Source H

A page from a thirteenth-century history. It shows the attack on Constantinople during the Fourth Crusade.

Source I

This eye-witness described the capture of Constantinople by crusaders during the Fourth Crusade.

'And certain people – who they were I know not – out of malice set fire to the city; and the fire waxed so great and horrible that no man could put it out. And when the leaders of the army . . . saw it they were filled with pity – seeing great churches and palaces falling in, and the great streets filled with merchandise burning in the flames.'

Geoffrey de Villehardouin, *The Conquest of Constantinople*, early thirteenth century

1 What explanation is given in Source A for the massacre of Jews?

2 There is evidence in this unit that suggests other possible explanations. Can you find that evidence?

3 Study Sources D, E and F. If Source F is reliable, can the other two sources also be reliable?

4 What difference would it make to your view of what happened in Jerusalem if you had only read Source F?

10 The Third Crusade

After the fall of Jerusalem during the First Crusade, the idea of crusading against unbelievers had taken a strong hold on the minds of Christians in Western Europe. Crusades were proclaimed against Muslims in Spain and Portugal, and pagans living in lands around the Baltic Sea. But in the East things had changed. Muslim forces grew stronger and more united and, in 1187, they recaptured Jerusalem.

How had the Muslim forces become stronger and what did Christians do about the loss of Jerusalem?

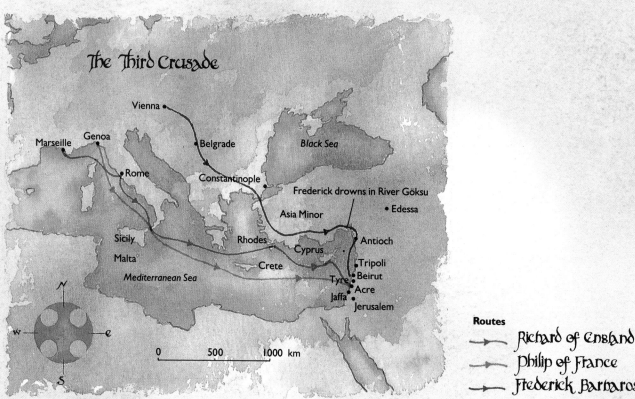

The Third Crusade

Vienna • Belgrade • Marseille • Genoa • Rome • Constantinople • Black Sea • Asia Minor • Frederick drowns in River Göksu • Edessa • Sicily • Rhodes • Cyprus • Antioch • Malta • Crete • Tripoli • Beirut • Mediterranean Sea • Tyre • Acre • Jaffa • Jerusalem

Routes

→ Richard of England
→ Philip of France
→ Frederick Barbarossa

0   500   1000 km

You will remember that when Jerusalem was captured by crusaders in 1099, the Muslim rulers in Palestine were weak from fighting each other. The new crusader states set up and ruled by the Christians were safe only while Muslim rulers remained weak. This was not to be for long.

The first sign of growing Muslim strength came in 1144 when the army of Imad al-Din Zangi captured Edessa from the crusaders. The Pope responded by proclaiming the Second Crusade, to recapture the city. Although it was led by the Kings of France and Germany, the Crusade failed to recapture Edessa.

Nur al-Din, son of Zangi, carried on the conquests of his father. He united many lands under his rule and surrounded the crusader states. On his death, in 1174, one of his generals, Saladin, became the Sultan.

Saladin, Salah al-Din Yusuf in Arabic, was a Kurd from northern Iraq. Here, historians are writing about what people thought of Saladin at the time.

Source A

'Those who knew Saladin say little about his physical appearance: he was small and frail, with a short, neat beard. They prefer to speak of his thoughtful and rather sad face, which would suddenly light up with a comforting smile that would put anyone talking to him at ease. He was always pleasant and friendly with visitors, insisting that they stay to eat, and treating them with full honours, even if they were infidels.'

Amin Maalouf, *The Crusades Through Arab Eyes,* 1983

Source B

'To his admirers, Saladin can be seen as the hero of Islam, the destroyer of the Christian States, but many Muslims at the time did not share this view of him. They have pictured him as manipulating Islam to win power for himself and his family and only then launching his costly adventure.'

M.C. Lyons and D.E.P. Jackson, *Saladin,* 1982

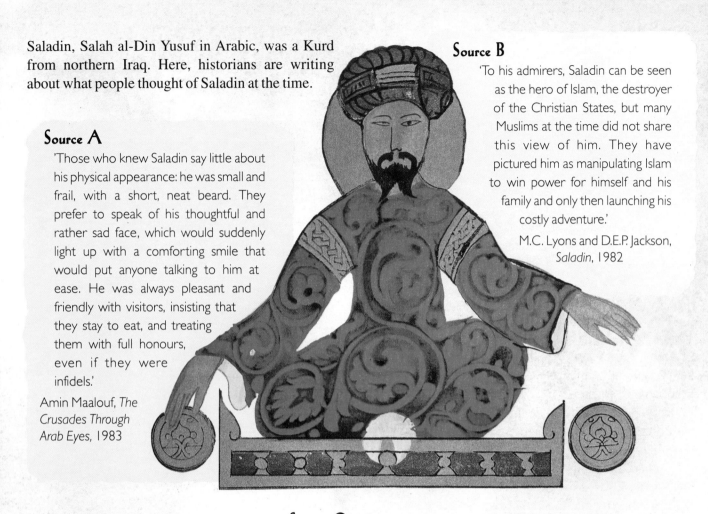

Source C ▲

This portrait of Saladin was painted by an Egyptian artist.
• *Does it support the description given in Source A?*

Saladin was soon ready to attack the crusader states. In 1187 he destroyed the army of the Kingdom of Jerusalem at the Battle of Hattin. In October of the same year, Jerusalem fell. By 1189 his army had captured over 50 crusader castles and nearly all the Kingdom of Jerusalem.

Source D ▼

The Battle of Hattin, 1187. Guy of Lusignan, King of Jerusalem, is shown fighting with Saladin. From the thirteenth-century chronicle of Matthew Paris.

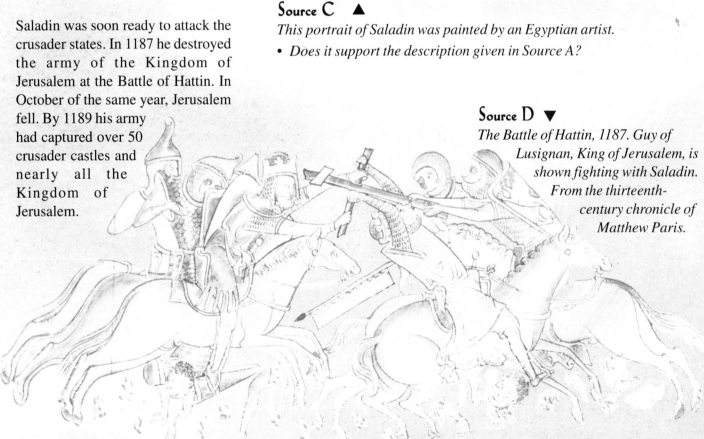

The news of the fall of Jerusalem shocked the Christian West. The Pope at the time, Urban III, is said to have died of shock. After the proclamation of the Third Crusade by the new Pope, Gregory VIII, three of the most powerful rulers in Europe took the cross: Frederick I Barbarossa ('Redbeard'), Emperor of Germany, Philip II of France, and Richard I of England, known as the Lionheart. Their aim was clear: to recapture Jerusalem.

The Emperor set out first at the head of a massive army. They marched across Europe and into Asia Minor where disaster struck. Frederick accidentally drowned when swimming in a river. Some of the army carried on, taking Frederick's body, pickled in vinegar, with them. But the German crusade was really over.

Richard and Philip now sailed for the Middle East. After landing they besieged the city of Acre and forced Saladin to make an agreement. By the agreement the Franks were to have the city and a large amount of gold. In exchange everyone in the city was to be allowed to go free. When the gold did not arrive on time, Richard ordered the massacre of nearly 3,000 prisoners who had been kept as hostages.

Philip, having had enough of crusading, had already left for France. Richard was now leading the crusade.

Source E

Frederick Barbarossa, Emperor of Germany, was 70 years old when he went on the Third Crusade. This picture of his coronation, 36 years before, shows how important crusading was at the time.

Source F

What was King Richard like? A modern historian gives this description.

'His courage and ability showed up best on the battlefield; he was a fine crusade commander and possibly the best of all. But he was also vain, with a love of pomp and display – he was very good-looking – and he was devious and self-centred.'

Jonathan Riley-Smith, *The Crusades*, 1987

In the next unit you will read accounts, written at the time, of what happened during the rest of the Third Crusade. Richard had many victories but he did not recapture Jerusalem. He made a peace with Saladin which allowed the Christians to keep land along the coast between the cities of Tyre and Jaffa. Muslims and Christians were to be free to travel throughout Palestine, including Jerusalem. However, Saladin's death, in March 1193, meant that the peace agreement did not last long.

In October 1192 Richard, who had been very ill, sailed for home. But he was not to reach there easily. Some of his actions during the crusade had angered other rulers in Europe and he was captured and imprisoned by Leopold of Austria. He spent nearly two years in prison before a ransom was paid and he was able to return to England.

1 The Battle of Hattin and the fall of Jerusalem to Saladin were short-term causes of the proclamation of the Third Crusade. What were some of the long-term causes?

2 Why did three of the most powerful rulers in Europe lead the Third Crusade? Describe, briefly, what happened to each of them.

3 Would you judge the Third Crusade to be a success?

4 Study Sources A, B and F.
a Make a list of the points made about Saladin and Richard I. Divide them into those you think are good points and those you think are bad points.
b Do you think all three sources are likely to be accurate? Explain your answer carefully.

5 Describe what seems to be happening in Source G. Do you think this actually happened? If not, what is the purpose of the tiles?

Source G
In these thirteenth-century tiles from Chertsey Abbey, King Richard I is shown charging at a Muslim horseman, probably meant to be Saladin.

11 The Third Crusade seen from different sides

To come as close as we can to the truth about the past or the present we need more than one version of what happened. Baha' ad-Din was an adviser to Saladin, and Ambroise was in the English army during the Third Crusade.

Both men wrote accounts of the same events, but are their versions the same?

The march from Acre to Arsuf (1191)

Source A – Ambroise

'Early in the morning the army was ready to advance along the sea coast in the name of the Lord. O what fine soldiers they were! Bright armour, pennons with their glittering emblazonry, banners, lances with gleaming points, shining helmets and coats of mail; an army terrible to the foe. The standard was formed of a long beam like the mast of a ship, made of solid timber and set on four wheels.'

Source B – Baha' ad-Din

'The enemy had already formed in order of battle; the infantry, drawn up in front of the cavalry, stood firm as a wall and every foot-soldier wore a vest of thick felt and a coat of mail so dense and strong that our arrows made no impression on them. I saw foot-soldiers with from one to ten arrows sticking in them, and still advancing at the ordinary pace without leaving the ranks. In the centre of their army was a cart, on which was fixed a tower as high as a minaret, and from this floated the standard of the people.'

After the battle of Arsuf (1191)

Source C – Ambroise

'The Sultan [Saladin], hearing that his best troops had been defeated by the Christians, was filled with anger and excitement. Calling together his emirs he said to them, "Are these the deeds of my brave troops, once so boastful?" One of them returned this answer: "We fought with all our strength and did our best but they are armed in armour which no weapon can pierce. Also there is one of them who is superior to any man we have ever seen: they call him Melek Ric [King Richard]. Such a king as he seems born to command the whole earth." '

Source D – Baha' ad-Din

'I stood beside him trying to console him; but he would not listen to me. God alone knows the depth of grief which filled his heart after this battle. There were a great number of killed and wounded this day on both sides. The Sultan's son, El-Afdal, charged so furiously that a growth he had in the face burst and he was drenched in blood. The soldiers from Mosul fought with the greatest bravery and won the Sultan's thanks.'

Source E
The seal of King Richard I.

- *What would this be used for?*

The crusaders (Franks) approach Jerusalem (1192)

Source F – Ambroise

'When news that King Richard was approaching was brought to those who lived in Jerusalem they were struck with terror. Not a man remained in the city and the Sultan himself demanded his swiftest horse so that he might flee from the face of King Richard, whose arrival he dared not wait.'

Source G – Baha' ad-Din

'On receiving this news the Sultan called his emirs together to discuss what should be done. It was decided that each emir should take charge of the defence of part of the walls of the city. He also decided to pollute all the water near the Holy City by stopping up the springs, destroying the cisterns and filling up the wells. He wanted to stay in the city but gave up this idea because of the great danger it might be for the cause of Islam.'

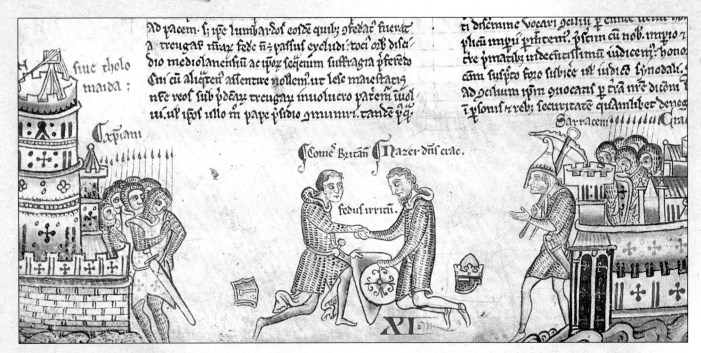

Source H
The thirteenth-century chronicle of Matthew Paris shows Richard the Lionheart and Saladin making a treaty. This meeting never took place.

The decision not to attack Jerusalem (1192)

Source I – Baha' ad-Din

'We have sent our spies to find out what is going on. On Saturday morning we received a message from a spy that the enemy is quarrelling. One group wants to attack the Holy City, the other wants to return to their own territory. The French insist on advancing towards Jerusalem and the King of England is against it. He says: "All the springs in the neighbourhood of the city have been polluted, so that there is not a drop of water to be had."'

Source J – Ambroise

'The French tried to persuade the king to lay siege to Jerusalem but he replied that it could not be done, saying, "Does not Saladin know all that goes on in our camp and do you think he does not know about our weak condition? He knows exactly what our strength is. If we attacked Jerusalem and should any misfortune happen while I was general (which God forbid), I alone would be blamed. This would bring ruin on my good name."'

Source K
The effigy of Richard I at Fontrevault in France.

• *Why do you think King Richard was buried in France?*

---

1 Study Sources A and B. Can you be certain that the two writers are describing the same scene?

2 Study Sources C and D.
a Do you think either writer has any purpose other than describing what happened?
b Do you trust one of the accounts more than the other? Explain your answer fully.

3 Study Sources F and G.
a What do the two versions agree on?
b What do they disagree on?

4 Study Sources I and J. Write your own version with the title 'The decision not to attack Jerusalem'. Base it on the two accounts but include only what you have worked out is probably reliable.

Fact or fiction?

Many stories have been written, pictures painted and television programmes and films made about the crusades.

Can we trust the ideas they give us about the past?

One of the most popular and powerful legends in England is that of Robin Hood. In the film *Robin Hood, Prince of Thieves*, there is one major change to the traditional story. As always, Robin returns from a crusade to the Holy Land to find his home and lands have been taken from him. His enemies are the friends of bad Prince John, who is ruling England while his brother, good King Richard, is on crusade. The difference is that this time Robin has a companion with him, a Muslim warrior, who fights by his side.

Source A
In the film Robin Hood, Prince of Thieves, *Robin returns from crusading in the Holy Land with a new companion.*

Source B
This picture of Richard the Lionheart was painted in the 1920s and hangs in the Houses of Parliament at Westminster.

Source C

In this story, Alec Bowden has found a beer-can made from metal that was melted down from an old lamp. In it is Abu Salem, a 975-year-old genie. One of the tasks Alec gives the genie to do for him is his history homework.

"'Ha, hm,' said Tweedy, and began to read. "When the galleys of the barbarians had broken through our ships, our Lord Sultan Salah ad-Din Yusuf, hammer of the infidel, called to him the emirs and took council with them.

His nephew, the bold warrior Taki, declared that the armies of the faithful should charge down upon the besiegers and sweep them into the sea. But his brother, the wise and wily Al-Adil, counselled caution. Only wait, said he, and the Frankish bandits would fall to quarrelling among themselves like the robbers they were."

Tweedy stopped reading and turned to the class. Some had started to laugh; others waited to see which way the cat would jump.

"And who, Mr Bowden," asked Tweedy, "was the chief of these Frankish bandits who quarrelled among themselves over the loot?"

Without thinking, Alec said, "King Richard."

"Not the same one we all used to know of as 'The Lion Hearted'," said Tweedy. "Aha, a completely new version of history. Fascinating." He bent over the desk. "And might I know from what source you obtained this picture?"

A sinking feeling gripped Alec's stomach. He couldn't very well say that a genie in a beer-can told him.'

Robert Leeson, *The Third Class Genie*, 1975

1 Do you think the purpose of the film (Source A) is to give an accurate picture of what it was like in England at the time of the Third Crusade? If not, what is the purpose of the film?

2 Why, in the film, might the story have been changed to include a Muslim warrior?

3 In Source C, why has the genie given a different version of history?

4 In the story the teacher, Tweedy, seems to think that 'different' means 'wrong'. What do *you* think?

5 The book, *The Third Class Genie*, is fiction. Does this mean we cannot trust it to help us know more about what the past was really like?

6 What opinion of King Richard does the artist of Source B want you to have?

7 Do you think the painting (Source B) is based on fact or has it come from the artist's imagination? Does your answer make a difference to how you view the picture?

The Hospitallers

The capture of Jerusalem by Saladin had shown how hard it was for the Christians to defend their conquests. Between crusades there were very few Christian soldiers to fight the increasingly strong Muslim armies. A permanent army of Christian knights was needed if the Holy Land was to be defended.

Who were these knights and how important were they?

Two military orders of 'religious' or monks became the defenders of the Holy Land. The first were the Knights of the Temple of Solomon, known as the Knights Templar. The second were the Knights of St John of Jerusalem, known as the Hospitallers. To understand the importance of these military orders, whose members were both monks and knights, we will look more closely at the Hospitallers.

Their story began in the eleventh century, before the First Crusade, when a group of monks built and ran a hospital for sick pilgrims in Jerusalem, near the Church of the Holy Sepulchre. It was called the hospital of St John of Jerusalem.

In the Middle Ages in Europe the main aim of the few hospitals that existed was to give good nursing care. It was thought that surgeons and physicians could only help in some cases and that most sick people would get better if they were given the right nursing care in the right conditions. The Hospitallers took these ideas to their hospital in Jerusalem.

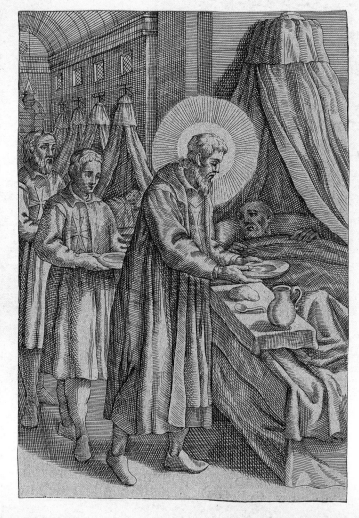

Source A

This sixteenth-century drawing shows brothers of the Order of St John nursing in the hospital in Malta. Malta was the headquarters of the Order from 1530 to 1798.

Source B

We can learn about the quality of nursing care given by the Hospitallers from their rules. As you read these extracts, remember what you have learned about the conditions in which poor people lived in the Middle Ages.

'Little cradles should be made for the babies of women pilgrims born in the House so that they may lie separate, and that the baby in its own bed may be in no danger from the restlessness of its mother.'

'Each bed should be covered with its own coverlet, and each bed should have its own special sheets.'

'For three days in the week the sick . . . have fresh meat, either pork or mutton, and those who are unable to eat it have chicken.'

'Guarding and watching them day and night, the brethren of the Hospital should serve the sick poor with zeal and devotion as if they were their lords . . . wash their feet gently, and change their sheets and make their beds.'

'Each of the sick should have a cloak of sheepskin and boots for going to and from the latrines, and caps of wool.'

'Violence is not always bad. For example, if a surgeon has to cut off someone's leg to save her or his life, that is a violent act but it is not a bad act. So it is not violence that is either good or bad, it is the purpose for which the violence is committed.'

'Violence can be good if it is used against those who stand in the way of the will of God.'

Source C
Fina, Prioress of England 1180–1240. Fina was the first Prioress of the Hospitaller nuns in England.

In 1113 the Pope recognised the Hospitallers as a new, separate order of monks and nuns: the Order of St John. Those who joined the Order took vows of poverty, chastity and obedience and their main task was to care for sick pilgrims and the sick poor. Before long, the Order built more hospitals in the crusader states and in Europe.

By the middle of the twelfth century, monks of the Order of St John were fighting as well as caring for the sick. They were both monks and knights: members of the military order of the Knights of St John. How was it possible to fight and carry out acts of violence, when holy vows had been taken to care for the sick? Here are two of the arguments that would have been used by the Knights of St John.

The Hospitaller castle of Krak des Chevaliers in Syria, first built in the twelfth century. The name means 'fortress of the knights'.

As the strength of the Muslim forces grew, the Hospitallers became increasingly involved in fighting to defend the Holy Places. They began to build castles as well as hospitals and it all had to be paid for. In Europe people gave land and money to the Hospitallers. So much was given that the Order of St John set up a huge organisation to look after all its land and wealth. Europe was divided into 25 different areas, each called a Priory. England, Wales and Scotland together made up one Priory and it was run by the Prior from the Order's headquarters at Clerkenwell in London.

The Order owned property in almost every county of England and Wales and the remains of much of it can still be seen today. So great was the wealth and power of the Order of St John that the Prior of England was very important in the country. Because he was Prior he was, by right, one of the main barons of England and, therefore, close to the throne.

Some Priors also held high positions in the government of the country. Here are some examples. The dates in brackets show when they were Prior of the Order of St John.

Robert (?) (1204–1214)	Treasurer of England
Joseph de Chauncey (1273–80)	Treasurer of England
Robert Hales (1371–81)	Treasurer of England
John Redington (1381–99)	Admiral of the King's Western Fleet
John Langstrother (1469–71)	Treasurer of England

In 1291 the last remaining area of Palestine still ruled by Christians was recaptured by a Muslim army. The Muslim victory was complete and the Knights of St John sailed away from the coast of Palestine for the last time. But the story of the Order of St John was far from over.

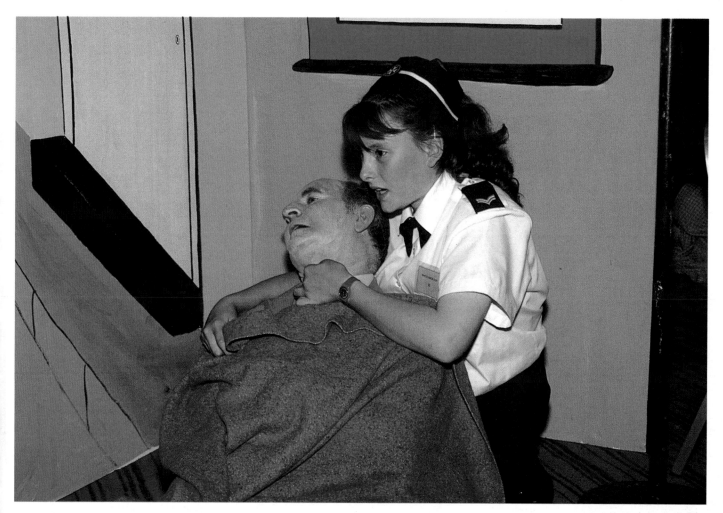

Source E

In the sixteenth century, King Henry VIII took away all the wealth, land and power of the Order of St John. But, in the nineteenth century, Queen Victoria agreed that the Order could return to England. Today, volunteers of St John Ambulance continue the nursing and caring traditions of the Hospitallers.

Source F

The crypt of the Priory Church of the Order of St John, at their headquarters in Clerkenwell, London. It was built by the Hospitallers in about 1140 and can still be visited today.

1 Draw a time-line and mark on it the centuries from AD 1000 to AD 2000. On the time-line show all the changes that have happened to the Order of St John over that time. Begin with building a hospital in Jerusalem and end with St John Ambulance. Remember to use the picture sources as well as the written pieces.

2 Study the nursing rules that the Order of St John followed in their hospitals in the Middle Ages (Source B).
a In what ways are hospitals today the same, and in what ways are they different?
b Why, if people knew about good nursing in the Middle Ages, did so few people receive it?
c What do you think of the arguments the Hospitallers would have used about violence?

3 In this unit you are told that the Order of St John was wealthy and powerful. What evidence can you find that this is true?

14 The crusades continue

The crusading movement was at its height in the 200 years after the proclamation of the First Crusade but it was not ended by the Muslim victory in Palestine in 1291.

What happened next, and was crusading still popular?

Pagans remained targets until there were too few left to fight. Crusades were also called against heretics, Christians who were accused of following false beliefs. The war against Muslims continued in the eastern Mediterranean region. In the fifteenth century, Muslims were driven out of Spain and were attacked in North Africa.

In the East a new Muslim power was growing in strength, the Ottoman Turks. In 1453 they captured Constantinople and were ready to strike deep into Europe. Crusades were once again preached and, although Constantinople was not recaptured, the Turkish advance was eventually halted.

Source A
The fall of Constantinople to Ottoman Turks in 1453. This picture is from a fifteenth-century French manuscript.

Source B

The Battle of Damietta during the Fifth Crusade, from the thirteenth-century chronicle of Matthew Paris, an English monk.

• *How does Matthew Paris show some of the things that really happened during the battle?*

Crusades were not, however, popular with every Christian and some spoke and wrote against them. Here are some examples of **criticisms** from the twelfth and thirteenth centuries, the years when the crusading movement was strongest.

† It is not in accordance with the Christian religion to shed blood in this way, even that of wicked infidels. For Christ did not act thus.

† We have a duty to defend ourselves against the Saracens (Muslims) when they attack us but we should not attack their lands or their persons when they leave us in peace.

† What is the point of this attack on the Saracens? They are not converted to Christianity by it but rather stirred up against the Christian faith.

† Fake prophets persuaded Christians with empty words . . . to set out against the Saracens to liberate Jerusalem . . . the inhabitants of nearly every region offered themselves up for destruction.

† It does not appear to be God's will that Christians should fight the Saracens in this way because of the misfortunes that God has allowed to happen to the Christians . . . How could the Lord have allowed Saladin to retake the land won with so much Christian blood?

Although there were such criticisms, the evidence shows that many more people were for than against crusades. Thousands continued to take part even though they probably knew how unpleasant and dangerous a time they were likely to have.

Source C

It was believed that some captured crusaders suffered this fate. What is happening to the man in this twelfth-century bible illustration?

It is the year 1213 and the Pope has proclaimed the Fifth Crusade. You hear that a close friend of yours is going to take the cross. You agree with those who criticise the crusades and you want to persuade your friend not to go. Write a letter giving all the reasons why you think she or he should not go. Make sure you tell your friend all the evidence you have about how unpleasant and dangerous going on crusade can be. Think about what you have learned about crusading to the East. The following points will help you:

- expense
- the distance from Western Europe to Palestine
- the type of land that has to be crossed
- problems with food and drink
- surprise attacks
- disease
- being under siege
- battles
- the effect on the family left behind

15 Crusaders— who were they?

Almost any Christian could choose to take a vow that made her or him a crusader, and once the vow had been taken it could not be broken without fear of punishment from the Church and from God. So although some who took the vow never actually went on crusade, most did.

What sort of people were they?

The Children's Crusade

- Cologne
- Marbach

Many died or left to return home.

Some reached Genoa. Most did not.

The children believed the sea would dry up and they could walk to Jerusalem.

Genoa

To Jerusalem (3,000 km)

Mediterranean Sea

0 km 100

Source A

In England, near the end of the twelfth century, lists were made of people who had made a crusader vow. A historian who has studied the records tells us that

'...in Lincolnshire they were nearly all poor and included a clerk, a smith, a skinner, a potter, a butcher and a vintner; 43 crusaders were to be found in Cornwall, including a tailor, a smith, a shoemaker, 2 chaplains, a merchant, a miller, 2 tanners and 2 women.'

Jonathan Riley-Smith, *What were the Crusades?*, 1977

Source B

It is also recorded that in the year 1250 a ship called the St Victor sailed from France to the East. It was carrying 453 crusaders.

'14 knights
90 retainers [servants of the knights]
7 clerics [ministers of the Church]
300 male commoners
42 female commoners (15 were with their husbands, 2 with their brothers and one with her father).'

Crusading families

In some families almost everyone, women and men, went on crusade. This commitment would then be carried from one family to another through marriage. Historians are finding evidence that it was often the women who most strongly believed in crusading and inspired their brothers, husbands and sons to go.

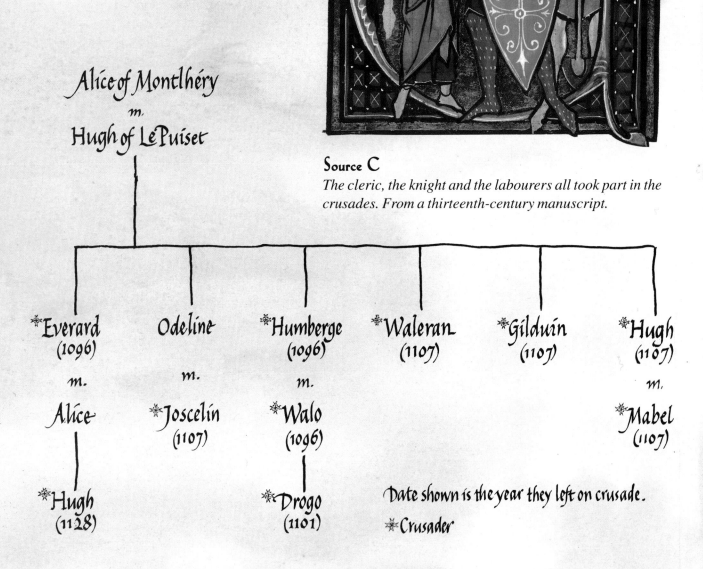

Source C
The cleric, the knight and the labourers all took part in the crusades. From a thirteenth-century manuscript.

Alice of Montlhéry
m.
Hugh of Le Puiset

*Everard (1096)	Odeline	*Humberge (1096)	*Waleran (1107)	*Gilduin (1107)	*Hugh (1107)
m.	m.	m.			m.
Alice	*Joscelin (1107)	*Walo (1096)			*Mabel (1107)
*Hugh (1128)		*Drogo (1101)			

Date shown is the year they left on crusade.
*Crusader

The Children's Crusade

The Third and Fourth Crusades were attempts to recapture Jerusalem after it had fallen to Saladin. They both failed and people searched for answers. Maybe God did not want Jerusalem to be recaptured by rich and powerful crusaders. Perhaps he wanted a different kind of person to crusade.

In Cologne, a large town in Germany, a 12-year-old boy called Nicholas claimed that God had called on him to lead children to Jerusalem and take it from the Muslims. The year was 1212 and thousands joined him on the 'Children's Crusade'.

The followers of the Children's Crusade headed south through Germany. They were aiming for Genoa, an Italian port. Here, Nicholas told them, the Mediterranean Sea would part and they would walk to Jerusalem. First they had to cross the Alps, the highest mountain range in Europe. Even though it was the summer it must have been difficult with very little food to eat. But most of the children survived this part of the journey.

Their worst troubles were only just beginning. Local people were now suspicious and not willing to help them. The summer was an unusually hot one and there had been a bad harvest. Many of the children died from the heat, or from lack of water and food. Many more gave up and tried to get home, struggling back over the Alps in winter.

Source G

The popular crusades, such as the Shepherds' Crusade, meant that thousands of people left the land.

• *What consequences could such crusades have?*

We do not know how many thousands left Germany with Nicholas but few returned, and no evidence has been found that any reached Palestine.

The story of the disappearing children changed, over time, from truth to fairy tale. The children are still remembered, although many who read 'The Pied Piper of Hamelin' may not know what they are really reading about.

Source H

The Children's Crusade was not the end of the idea of 'People's Crusades'. An Englishman wrote this about a Shepherds' Crusade.

'There was a 60-year-old Hungarian . . . This impostor . . . wandered about everywhere . . . falsely claiming that he had received an order from the Blessed Mary, the mother of the Lord, to summon shepherds and herdsmen . . . he said that heaven had granted them in their simplicity the privilege of recovering the Holy Land . . . they gradually began to follow him, leaving their flocks and herds without asking their lords or relatives and without bothering about what they would eat . . . their numbers greatly multiplied to . . . 100,000 or more.'

Chronicle of Matthew Paris, 1251

1 Based on the evidence in the sources decide whether each of the statements below is either certainly true or possibly true. Draw a chart and complete it by filling in the reason for your choice.
• Sometimes a mother, father and son went on crusade together.
• Knights were well looked after when they went by sea.
• At the end of the twelfth century 43 crusaders left Cornwall.
• Some women went on crusade on their own.
• No knights went on crusade from Lincolnshire at the end of the twelfth century.

2 Work in pairs and compare Sources D and H. What similarities can you find between the Children's Crusade and the Shepherds' Crusade? Are there any differences?

3 Tell the story of the Children's Crusade. It can be in any form you choose – drawings, a short story, poem, or letter – but make sure it is based on evidence.

16 | Motives for crusading

You have learned about how difficult and unpleasant going on crusade usually was. Yet people went in their thousands.

Why did they do it?

Why did Pope Urban II proclaim the First Crusade?

- To recover Jerusalem.
- To make it safe for Christian pilgrims to travel to holy places.
- To defend the Eastern Christians of the Byzantine Empire.
- To give the Church more authority and influence in people's lives.
- To involve people in pilgrimages to change the way they behaved.
- To acquire land.

These reasons help to explain why Pope Urban wanted crusades against Muslims but they do not explain why so many people went on crusades. To understand more about why people do things, we need to find out about their beliefs. One of the main teachings of the Christian Church in the Middle Ages was that God saw everything and knew everything. Sins could not be hidden and when a person died God would judge her or him and penalties would have to be paid for all the sins that had been committed.

Think about these beliefs when you study the sources of evidence about people's motives for going on crusades.

Source A

An image of hell, or purgatory, from the twelfth century.

- *How would you describe what is happening?*

55

Source B

'I, Nivelo . . . had harshly worn down the land of the Abbey of St Peter by seizing the goods of the inhabitants there. In order to obtain the pardon for my crimes which God can give me, I am going on a crusade to Jerusalem.'

From a charter to the abbey of St Peter of Chartres, written for Nivelo of Freteval, 1096

Source C

'. . . we give to these military men who are fit to defend the Holy Land and go to these Holy Places . . . and fight there for two years against the Saracens . . . absolution from all the crimes of which they make confession . . . We allow all those willing to visit the Lord's Sepulchre . . . whether they die on the journey or reach that place to count this journey as penance and an act of obedience to the Church and for the remission of all sins.'

From a letter of Pope Alexander III, 1181

Source D

'All who should take the cross and serve . . . for one year would be delivered from all the sins they had committed and acknowledged in confession. And because this indulgence was so great, the hearts of men were much moved, and many took the cross for the greatness of the pardon.'

Geoffrey of Villehardouin, *The Conquest of Constantinople,* early thirteenth century

Source E
One of many medieval pictures drawn to show people what they could suffer in hell, about 1400.

---

1 Use the sources in this unit to work out what Christians were taught about the after-life in the Middle Ages.

2 What did Nivelo hope to get from God by going on crusade?

3 What exactly did people have to do to gain the pardon promised by Pope Alexander III?

4 Had any new promises been made to crusaders by the time Villehardouin wrote his chronicle (Source D)? If so, why do you think the promises had changed?

5 Write two paragraphs about motives for going on crusade. In the first one try and think as someone at the time might have thought. In the second paragraph give your own opinion of the motives.

Historians

Historians try to get as close to the truth about events in the past as possible.

But do they all agree on what happened and why?

These sources summarise the views of different historians writing about why people went on the First Crusade.

Source A – Abba Eban

'The First Crusade was supposed to be a religious war to free the Holy Land from Muslim control. Many people were ready to fight simply for this purpose, but others had different motives. To Pope Urban II it was a chance to show his leadership over European Christendom. To the knights, it was a chance for adventure, looting and conquest. To the merchants of Italy, it meant re-opening trade routes in the East that had been blocked by the Muslims. So there were mixed motives in the crusader armies: religion, power and greed.'

Source B – Hans Mayer

'In some parts of western Europe knights had started to practise the system of primogeniture. This means that, on the death of the father, all his land and wealth is passed on to the eldest son. Younger sons had to look after themselves. The crusades gave these younger sons something to do with their lives and, perhaps, a chance to become independent.'

Source C – Jonathan Riley-Smith

'Reading the charters makes one thing clear. Family land was often sold or mortgaged to provide crusaders with money. There is very little evidence to support the view that the crusade was an opportunity for spare sons to find something to do. Instead it points to families raising money and taking on burdens to help members carry out their crusader vows. It makes sense, therefore, to suppose that the motive was a strong belief in crusading.'

Source D

The capture of Antioch in 1098 during the First Crusade. This was such a surprising victory that many of the crusaders thought it showed God was supporting their cause. Historians now disagree about the knights' reasons for going on crusade.

1 Each historian has views about the motives of the crusaders.
a Can you find any agreement between the views of the three different historians?
b What do they disagree about?

2 What evidence is used in Source C that is not used in Source B? Do you think Hans Mayer would have had a different view if he had known the evidence in Source C?

3 You have only been given a small part of what each historian wrote. Does this matter?

4 Which of the three sources do you find most convincing? Are there any questions you would like to ask the historians before you make your mind up?

The legacy of the crusades

The crusades made a difference to the lives of millions of people at the time when they were happening, and many things changed because they happened. Some of those changes still have consequences in our world today.

What changed because of the crusades and what difference have they made to the past and the present?

The Arab and Islamic worlds have played an important part in shaping Europe as it is today. In the Middle Ages, Arab music and literature and Muslim learning had a great influence on Europeans. Muslim scholars were particularly advanced in mathematics, astronomy, medicine, geography, chemistry and architecture.

Many of the Arabic words that have become part of the English language are clues to what was learned. Here are just some of those beginning with '**a**'.

admiral alcohol alcove algebra
alkali arsenal atlas average

Much of the exchange of ideas and learning between Muslims and Christians came about because of the long presence of Arabs in Spain and Sicily. The crusades and the Christian settlements in the East brought contact of a different kind between the two religions and added some new knowledge, although not very much. So what difference did the crusades make?

Source A
There were observatories for studying the stars in many Muslim cities in the Middle Ages. Here, scientists are shown at work in an observatory.

In this book you have looked at some of the short-term results of the many crusades. Now think about the points that people have made about how the crusades continued to make a difference after they ended.

- Even today many Europeans have an image of Muslims that comes from the time of the crusades. This means it is a false or distorted image.

- Crusading to the East made West Europeans realise that there were other states beyond the Islamic states. This helped to bring about the explorations which eventually led to the discovery of America.

- Income tax was first introduced to pay for the crusades.

- You need to study the crusades if you want to try to understand today's conflict in the Middle East. The Christian crusaders slaughtered Muslims and Jews in their holy wars, and Muslims killed Christians. Even now, it is difficult for Christians, Jews and Muslims to live peacefully side by side.

- The crusades were the first example of West Europeans setting out to conquer and colonise other parts of the world. Many people in the Middle East know that their ancestors were victims of Westerners during the crusades, and want to make sure they are never victims again. This means they still see the West as an enemy.

- Even though they failed, the crusades gave West Europeans an image of themselves as powerful fighters for Christ. They went on to dominate the world.

- In some parts of Europe the holy wars of the Middle Ages live on. For example, some of the causes of fighting earlier this century between Poles, Germans and Russians can be traced back to the crusades. The same is true of fighting between Serbs, Croats and Bosnians.

Source B

This map of the world was produced in 1154 by al-Idrisi, a Muslim cartographer [map maker].

- *How good a map do you think it is?*

1 Write out the list of words taken from Arabic on page 60 and a list of the subjects Muslim scholars were advanced in. Show which subject each word is connected to.

2 Why did the crusades not make much difference to what Muslims and Christians learned from each other?

3 Think back over what you have learned and, if you need to, look back through the book. Give three short-term results of the First Crusade and three short-term results of the Third Crusade.

4 Put each of the long-term results given in this unit under the heading (below) which you think fits it best. If you prefer, you can make up your own headings.

- To do with views people have about each other.

- To do with how the crusades changed Western Europe.

- To do with how the crusades changed the world.

Attainment Target Grid

This grid is designed to indicate the varying emphases on attainment targets in the questions in each unit. It is not to be interpreted as a rigid framework, but as a simple device to help the teacher plan the study unit.

X   some focus

XX   strong focus

XXX   main focus

		AT1			AT2	AT3
		a	**b**	**c**		
1	Jerusalem – Holy City	*X*	*XXX*			
2	Changes in the East	*X*				*XXX*
3	Changes in the West			*XX*		*XXX*
4	Crusading is launched		*XXX*			*XX*
5	The First Crusade	*X*		*XX*		*XXX*
6	The crusader states	*XX*			*XX*	*XXX*
7	The call to crusade		*XXX*	*X*		*XX*
8	Leaving home			*XX*	*XXX*	*XX*
9	Victims of crusades		*XXX*		*XX*	*XX*
10	The Third Crusade		*XX*	*XXX*	*XXX*	*X*
11	The Third Crusade seen from different sides		*XX*			*XXX*
12	Fact or fiction?				*XXX*	
13	The Hospitallers	*XXX*		*XX*		*X*
14	The crusades continue		*XXX*			
15	Crusaders – who were they?		*XXX*			*XX*
16	Motives for crusading		*XX*	*XXX*		*X*
17	Historians				*XXX*	
18	The legacy of the crusades		*XXX*	*X*		

Attainment Target Focus

Index